TIME FOR KIDS

A Visit to a Publisher

D. M. Rice

Table of Contents

The Publisher

I am a lot like my mom. We both love to write!

I am writing about baseball. When I am finished, I will give the story to my mom.

My mom is an **editor**. She works for a magazine publisher.

Maybe they will print my story in their magazine!

The magazine offices are fun to visit. They are high up in a skyscraper in the middle of the city.

When we go there, the doorman winks at me and asks, "Are you working here today?" I laugh and go inside.

Did You Know?

Editors make choices about what goes in a magazine. They also make sure that the writing is the best it can be.

TIME & LIFE

Did You Know?

An **issue** means a copy of a magazine for a new week.

Then up the elevator we go. When the doors open, we see people rushing back and forth. They work fast to publish the magazine.

Each week they must finish a new **issue**. They can't be late! Their readers expect a new magazine. They expect it on time. They expect it to be good!

Making a Magazine

When it is time for a new issue, the editors have a big meeting. They choose the magazine **articles**. They also choose the story writers.

Did You Know?

Article is another word for a magazine story.

The writers make the stories interesting to read.

Magazines need pictures, too. Photographers take the pictures, or artists may draw them.

Next, designers get to work. They put the writing and pictures together on the magazine pages.

TIME
SHARKS!
Spiders Grow Up
TIME

Ready for Print

Everyone works fast! When they are finished, the editors check their work.

Is everything ready? Yes, it is! So, now it is time for printing.

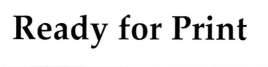

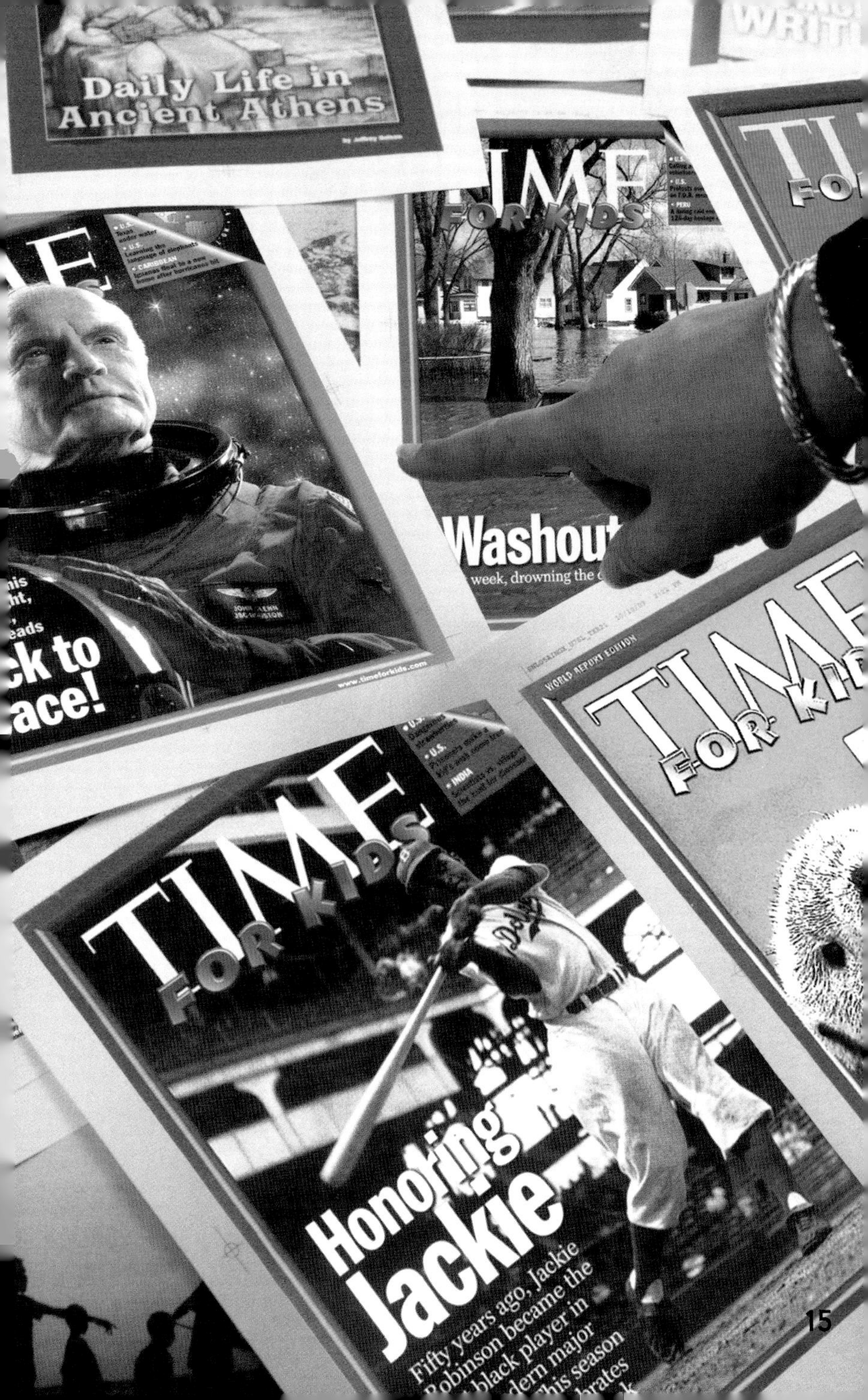
Daily Life in Ancient Athens
TIME FOR KIDS
Washout
www.timeforkids.com
WORLD REPORT EDITION
Honoring Jackie
Fifty years ago, Jackie Robinson became the

The printing factory is large and noisy. Huge rolls of paper are fed into printing machines. The machines print, cut, and staple the magazines.

“Ready for delivery!” the printer calls.

Then big mail trucks take them away.

Ready for Reading

Some magazines come in the mail. Some magazines are bought in stores. You can even find magazines at the library.

The next time you read a magazine, maybe you will see my story there!

Publishing a Magazine

How is a magazine published? This chart will show you.

Editors choose the story ideas.

Writers write the stories.

Photographers and artists take and draw pictures for the stories.

Designers put the writing and pictures together on the pages.

Editors check everything.

The printing factory prints the magazine.

Mail trucks bring the magazines to the readers.

Glossary

artist person who draws pictures for a magazine

designers people who decide how a magazine should look

editor person who decides what should go in a magazine and makes sure it has no mistakes

photographer person who takes photographs for magazine stories

printing factory company that prints a magazine for people to read

publisher company that hires people to create a magazine

writer person who writes stories for a magazine